This book belongs to

Cheyenne A. Randolph

# THE SANDMAN
## and
## Other Sleepy-Time Rhymes

Illustrated by

Judy Mastrangelo

The Unicorn Publishing House
New Jersey

# The Sandman

The Sandman's coming, *soft and low,*
Coming from Sleepy Town careful and slow;
Riding on moonbeams silvery bright,
Have you *ever* seen such a marvelous sight!

The Sandman's coming, *soft and low,*
Bringing sweet dreams that each child knows;
Tucked in his sack, brimming with sand,
He flies through the clouds as fast as he can.

The Sandman's coming, *soft and sweet,*
When night has fallen, and it's time to sleep;
Then silently creeping close by your side,
He'll sprinkle his magic, two grains in your eyes.

Has the Sandman come to you, little one,
    Now that your busy day is done?
How will you know that he has been there—
    This clever fellow as light as air?

You will know, my dear, when first you yawn,
That, indeed, the Sandman has come and gone;
And as you rub each tired eye,
Two grains of dream sand you shall spy.

So lay your head down softly, my sweet,
And journey on to the Land of Sleep;
Snug and warm - safe from harm,
Dream sweet dreams until the dawn.

*Adapted from a German Lullaby*

# The Fly-Away Horse

Oh, a wonderful horse is the Fly-Away Horse—
    Perhaps you have seen him before;
Perhaps, while you slept, his shadow has swept
    Through the moonlight that floats on the floor.
For it's only at night, when the stars twinkle bright,
    That the Fly-Away Horse, with a neigh
And a pull at his rein and a toss of his mane,
    Is up on his heels and away!
        The Moon in the sky,
        As he gallops by,
      Cries: "Oh! what a marvelous sight!"
        The Stars stop their play
        Hide their faces away
    In the lap of old Grandmother Night.

It is yonder, out yonder, the Fly-Away Horse
 Speeds ever and ever away—
Over meadows and lanes, over mountains and plains,
 Over streams that sing at their play;
And over the sea like a ghost sweeps he,
 While the ships they go sailing below,

But tell us, my dear, all you see and you hear
   In those beautiful lands over there,
Where the Fly-Away Horse wings his far-away course
   With the wee one assigned to his care.
      Then grandma will cry
      In amazement: "Oh, my!"
  And she'll think it could never be so;
      And only we two
      Shall know it is true—
You and I, little precious! shall know!

*Adapted from a poem by Eugene Field*

Off! scamper to bed—you shall ride him to-night!
    For, as soon as you've fallen asleep,
With a jubilant neigh he shall bear you away
    Over forest and hillside and deep!

And the Fly-Away Horse seeks those far-away lands
    You little folk dream of at night—
Where candy-trees grow, and honey-brooks flow,
    And corn-fields with popcorn are white;
And the beasts in the wood are ever so good
    To children who visit them there—
What glory to ride a lion so fair,
    Or to wrestle around with a bear!
        The monkeys, they say:
        "Come on, let us play,"
    And they frisk in the cocoanut-trees:
        While the parrots, that cling
        To the peanut-vines, sing
    And fan a cool wind with their wings!

And he speeds so fast that the men at the mast
Think him some terrible soul.
"What ho there!" they cry,
As he flourishes by
With a whisk of his beautiful tail;
And the fish in the sea
Are as scared as can be,
From the nautilus up to the whale!

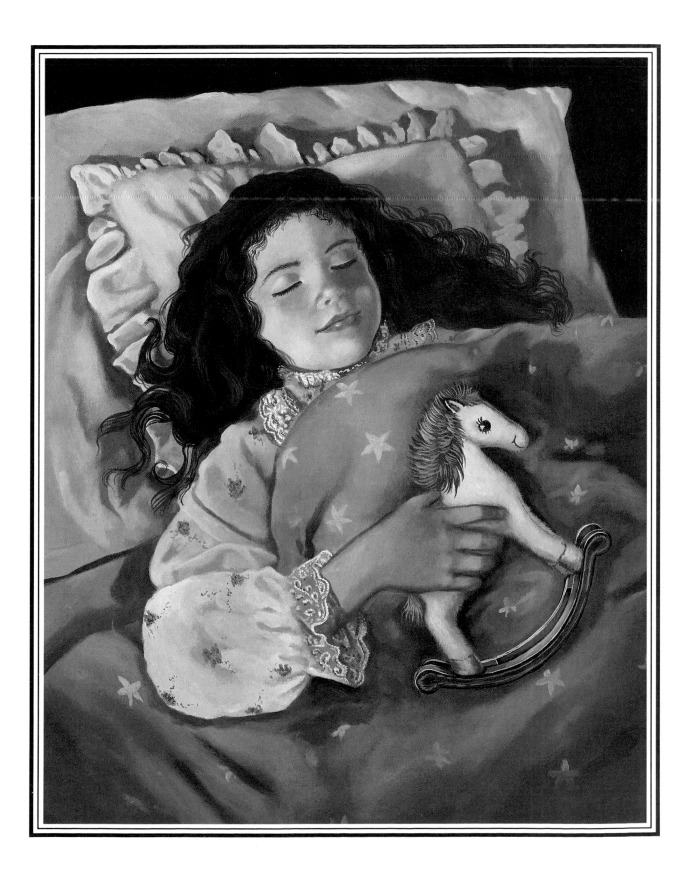

# The Rock-a-By Lady

The Rock-a-By Lady from Hushaby street
    Comes stealing; comes creeping;
The poppies they hang from her head to her feet,
And each hath a dream that is tiny and fleet—
She bringeth her poppies to you, my sweet,
    When she findeth you sleeping!

There is one little dream of a beautiful drum—
    "Rub-a-dub!" it goeth;
There is one little dream of a big sugar-plum,
And lo! thick and fast the other dreams come
Of popguns that bang, and tin tops that hum,
    And a trumpet that bloweth!

And dollies peep out of those wee little dreams
　　　With laughter and singing;
And the boats go a-floating on silvery streams,
And the stars peek-a-boo with their own misty gleams,
And up, up, and up, where the Mother Moon beams,
　　　The fairies go winging!

Would you dream all these dreams—
    That are tiny and fleet?
    They'll come to you sleeping;
So shut the two eyes that are weary, my sweet,
For the Rock-a-By Lady from Hushaby street,
With poppies that hang from her head to her feet,
    Comes stealing; comes creeping.

*Eugene Field*

# Young Night Thought

All night long and every night,
　　When my mama puts out the light,
I see the people marching by,
　　As plain as day, before my eye.

Armies and emperors and kings,
  All carrying different kinds of things,
And marching in so grand a way,
  You never saw the like by day.

So fine a show was never seen
    At the great circus on the green;
For every kind of beast and man
    Is marching in that caravan.

At first they move a little slow,
    But still the faster on they go,
And still beside them close I keep
    Until we reach the town of Sleep.

*Anonymous*

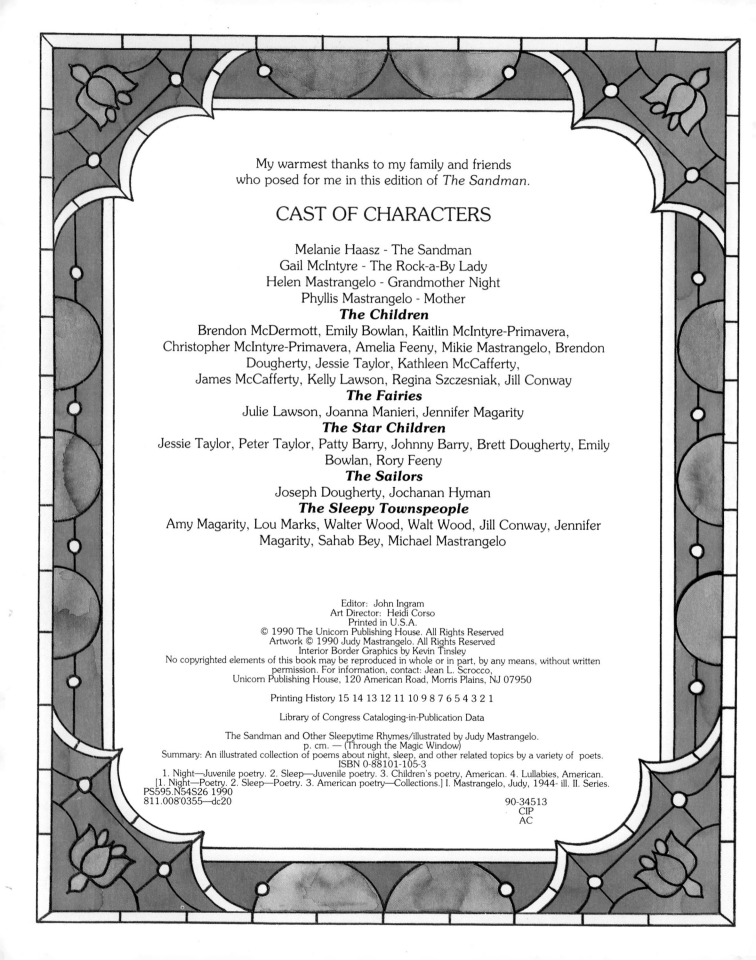

My warmest thanks to my family and friends
who posed for me in this edition of *The Sandman*.

## CAST OF CHARACTERS

Melanie Haasz - The Sandman
Gail McIntyre - The Rock-a-By Lady
Helen Mastrangelo - Grandmother Night
Phyllis Mastrangelo - Mother
### *The Children*
Brendon McDermott, Emily Bowlan, Kaitlin McIntyre-Primavera,
Christopher McIntyre-Primavera, Amelia Feeny, Mikie Mastrangelo, Brendon
Dougherty, Jessie Taylor, Kathleen McCafferty,
James McCafferty, Kelly Lawson, Regina Szczesniak, Jill Conway
### *The Fairies*
Julie Lawson, Joanna Manieri, Jennifer Magarity
### *The Star Children*
Jessie Taylor, Peter Taylor, Patty Barry, Johnny Barry, Brett Dougherty, Emily
Bowlan, Rory Feeny
### *The Sailors*
Joseph Dougherty, Jochanan Hyman
### *The Sleepy Townspeople*
Amy Magarity, Lou Marks, Walter Wood, Walt Wood, Jill Conway, Jennifer
Magarity, Sahab Bey, Michael Mastrangelo

Editor:  John Ingram
Art Director:  Heidi Corso
Printed in U.S.A.
© 1990 The Unicorn Publishing House. All Rights Reserved
Artwork © 1990 Judy Mastrangelo. All Rights Reserved
Interior Border Graphics by Kevin Tinsley
No copyrighted elements of this book may be reproduced in whole or in part, by any means, without written
permission. For information, contact: Jean L. Scrocco,
Unicorn Publishing House, 120 American Road, Morris Plains, NJ 07950

Printing History 15 14 13 12 11 10 9 8 7 6 5 4 3 2 1

Library of Congress Cataloging-in-Publication Data

The Sandman and Other Sleepytime Rhymes/illustrated by Judy Mastrangelo.
p. cm. — (Through the Magic Window)
Summary: An illustrated collection of poems about night, sleep, and other related topics by a variety of  poets.
ISBN 0-88101-105-3
1. Night—Juvenile poetry. 2. Sleep—Juvenile poetry. 3. Children's poetry, American. 4. Lullabies, American.
[1. Night—Poetry. 2. Sleep—Poetry. 3. American poetry—Collections.] I. Mastrangelo, Judy, 1944- ill. II. Series.
PS595.N54S26 1990
811.008'0355—dc20
90-34513
CIP
AC

For over a decade,
Unicorn has been publishing
richly illustrated editions of classic and
contemporary works for children and adults.
To continue this tradition, WE WOULD LIKE
TO KNOW WHAT YOU THINK.

If you would like to send us your suggestions
or obtain a list of our current titles,
please write to:
THE UNICORN PUBLISHING HOUSE, INC.
P.O.Box 377
Morris Plains, NJ   07950
ATT: Dept CLP